'Nashvi
of the North'

Country Music
In Liverpool

Kevin McManus

© Institute of Popular Music
University of Liverpool
Post Office Box 147
Liverpool L69 3BX

First published in Great Britain in 1994
ISBN 1 898806004

CONTENTS

Foreward

Acknowledgment

FOREWORD

People often talk of a "Liverpool Sound," though there are of course many different Liverpool Sounds whether they be sea shanties or football chants, doo wop and swing bands, or the numerous other musical forms and styles that shape the city's rich and diverse musical heritage.

This series is based on a three-year oral history project conducted by researchers from the Institute of Popular Music at the University of Liverpool. The research was made possible by a grant from the Leverhulme Trust, and we would like to thank the Trust for its generous support.

Sara Cohen
Senior Research Fellow
Institute of Popular Music

ACKNOWLEDGMENT

The information for this study was gathered mainly by means of interviews with country musicians and fans. Thanks are due to everyone who participated.

While I have tried to be as comprehensive as possible, it was impractical to attempt to interview, or even mention, the vast number of people and bands associated with the country music scene in Liverpool over the last thirty years. The stories told here are just a sample.

Special thanks are due to Hank Walters, Tony Allen, Bernie Green, Frances Hunt, Carmel Farley, Bunter Perkins, and Mick O'Toole, who went out of their way to be of assistance.

Archive material (records, newspaper articles, photographs,) was gathered from many sources, and thanks are due to everybody who made material available.

I have attempted to corroborate oral evidence as much as possible, but when people are relying on memories of events which took place up to forty years ago, some inaccuracies are bound to slip in (particularly when much of the information is anecdotal in nature). Hopefully these are few and will be overshadowed by fond memories provoked by these stories of Liverpool Country's early years.

Kevin McManus

'Talk About Country!' Hank Walters and the Dusty Road Ramblers at the Cavern, circa 1958.

Country music first began to emerge as a distinct commercial genre in the Southern states of 1920s America with the rise of musicians like Jimmie Rodgers, often regarded as "The Father of Modern Country." It flourished during the 1930s on radio barn dances and grew even more popular during the 1940s and 1950s with the emergence of stars such as Ernest Tubb, Hank Williams, Elvis Presley and Johnny Cash. Since then, country has spawned a host of household names including Patsy Cline, Tammy Wynette, Willie Nelson and Dolly Parton.

If we go further back we find that hillbilly music evolved out of a reservoir of folksongs, ballads and instrumental pieces brought to North America by the Anglo Celtic immigrants. It gradually absorbed influences from other musical sources, including the culture of African Americans, and in the socially conservative South, especially around the Appalachian Mountain region, a music emerged from the area's folk culture. This was the beginning of country music.

It is generally accepted that the first British country music emerged from Liverpool. How did this music from the "hillbilly" Southern states of America become so popular in a British city?

Joe Butler, who has played in country bands in Liverpool since 1958 and hosted a popular country music radio show for twenty years, offers the most widely accepted view.

"Liverpool is known to this day as the biggest place for country in Britain. At the time we started, there was no country anywhere else at all. A lot of it had to do with the fact that Liverpool is a seaport and people could get friends or relatives on ships to bring records home from the States that you couldn't get in the UK. You still get records brought back from the States that way."

This is a view reinforced by Hank Walters, a retired docker who is generally regarded as The Father of Liverpool Country.

"In Liverpool at the time (1950s and '60s) there was a massive merchant navy community that went to the States. We used to call them Cunard Yanks. A Cunard Yank was a guy who went to the States for ten days and

1

The Blue Mountain Boys at the Everton Valley Social Club, circa 1958.

came back with an American accent, loud ties and a baseball cap. But they also brought records back with them."

Kevin McGarry, lead singer with The Hillsiders, explains what happened to the records brought home by the local seamen.

"Hardly any people today will still have the old country records because one album would do five or six streets. Someone would get it and say 'have you heard this Hank Snow album?' and it would get passed around."

So the fact that Liverpool was the direct route for shipping traffic from America clearly had a great deal to do with why country music emerged there first. Additionally, the fact that the city was a port ensured that Liverpool was a cosmopolitan, open-minded place receptive to new ideas and new musics. The sea also offered local people the prospect of employment and the chance to broaden their horizons. As Kenny Johnson (another long-established musician and country DJ) puts it: "It was the same reason as why Merseybeat started here; because of the seamen. We used to get the soul records and the rock and roll records long before anyone else got them just because we were here and the sailors would bring them."

Carl Goldby (usually called "Goldie" in country music circles), another important figure in this history, bought his first guitar while on a voyage to

2

New Zealand and learned to play it on board ship. Bunter Perkins, stalwart of The Blue Mountain Boys, was a ship's cook. He also bought his first guitar in New Zealand after a voyage on *The Tamorowa*.

Hank Walters, who spent most of his working life on the docks, traces the Cajun influence in his music back to his grandfather who jumped ship (the *Alice Aleigh*, the biggest sailing ship ever to sail out of Liverpool) and lived for a while in Louisiana.

Tony Allen, the original lead singer with The Blue Mountain Boys, remembers getting his first country records off his older brother, who was a merchant seaman. Later, when he went to sea himself, he was taught to play guitar while on board ship.

Bernie Green, Allen's replacement in The Blue Mountain Boys, left country music for almost a decade at one point in his career to work on the North Sea before he was drawn back into country.

"The bug came back through listening to music on board. They were all lads from the Southern states, so they were very country oriented. We had a few jam sessions and then I got the urge again and came back to it."

Joe Butler points out a second possible factor in why country music took

The Blue Mountain Boys with Bernie Green at the Crazy Horse Saloon, Butlins, Clacton on Sea, 1963

3

off in Liverpool, citing further American influences from the neighbouring Burtonwood American Air Base.

"They used to have country on regularly there. They used to bring bands in from the States and various musicians went into the base. That and sailors bringing records home from the States were the biggest factors as to why it started in Liverpool."

Hank Walters, Kenny Johnson and Bernie Green all played at Burtonwood. Johnson remembers the jukebox there featured the likes of Ernest Tubb, Webb Pierce and Hank Williams.

Green recalls being asked to play at the base sometime around the mid-1950s.

"We (The Drifting Cowboys) were approached by the staff sergeant from Burtonwood. He took us to the base and we ended up playing there about twice a week for the following four years in the Servicemen's Club— one night in the GI club and one night in the officer's mess. We must have been doing something right because we were there for three or four years. At the time (the U.S. airmen) couldn't believe it because we sang in an American style. We got on like a house afire. They in their turn gave us a load of records, so the learning material was endless. It helped us enormously. We might be getting say £10 local but when we went to play for them we were getting three times that amount and all you could eat."

So Liverpool's early pre-eminence in British country music could be explained to a large extent by the city's unique position as a port trading with the United States, and to a lesser extent by the proximity of Burtonwood Air Base. On the other hand it could be something much simpler:

"Country music could be sung by a whole load of people, and that's what they like here." (Hank Walters)

4

It is generally agreed that the first groups playing country music in Liverpool were Hank Walters and The Dusty Road Ramblers, The Drifting Cowboys (featuring Bernie Green), Phil Brady's Ranchers, and Cyl Con and The Westernaires. Many of the musicians involved in these seminal groups are still playing today, emphasising the continuity which seems to be a feature of the Liverpool country scene.

There is some debate as to who was actually the first to play country music in the city. It's the sort of debate that rages at the end of a long night in a pub when several country musicians are gathered, but in the sober light of day the people debating loudest would probably agree that it doesn't really matter.

Tony Barnes, a local enthusiast who was around in the very early days, sums up the situation at the time:

"Hank (Walters) was probably going, but only playing local in his own area, and known only to his own area. At the same time, Bernie Green was only known in his own area. I knew the Miller Brothers because they were in my area. When people branched out and into Liverpool we all got to know each other."

Bernie Green himself is not keen to get into an argument about it.

"Hank Walters contacted me. He said, 'I've heard you're in a country band' and we arranged to meet at The Blue House. That was the first time I met him and he already had a band established. There was always some debate as to whether he'd been first or I'd been first, but it doesn't really matter because it just means whoever was first is the eldest. Anyway, we became staunch friends from that day and I was to join his band at a later day."

Walters is rather more dogmatic on the question of who was first.

"I started country music off in Liverpool. I don't know of any other country bands as such that were around before me. If you go to Vienna Street School, you'd find in the records that I had a band in that school when I was 13 (Spike Walters and the Hillbillies). Bernie Green (54 years old) is about five years younger, so I've got to be ahead of him (Hank is

5

Tony Barnes, compere at the Black Cat, 1992. (photo F. Hunt)

now 60). If you look at the adverts in the paper you'll find my name well ahead of anyone else in Liverpool, before The Beatles or anyone."

Hank's first country band was formed when he came out of the army in 1953.

"I came home on the 18th of October and started on the docks on the 20th of October. On the first day there, there was a bloke on the stairs playing the accordion and he knew I could play one. That was Mike King and he came along and asked me what I was doing that night. 'Can we come up to your house and have a rehearsal?' He came with Billy Whitty and they played a tune on guitars and they eventually got around me. Before I knew it, Hank Walters and The Dusty Road Ramblers were going. So I had Billy Whitty and Mike King on the instruments and then we were joined by a fella called Bob Crawford on harmonica. Alongside of him was Jimmy Duncan and Johnny Slater. Later on I brought in a bass player called Eddie Clayton. That was between 1953 and 1957."

Hank (whose real name is William Ralph Walters) gained his nickname because of his great affection for Hank Williams and he clearly remembers the first time he heard a record by the legendary country artist.

"I heard Hank Williams in 1949 (when Walters was 16) in a place called The Blue Bell Cafe (in Aintree). They had a jukebox and on it was 'Wedding Bells'/'Lovesick Blues'. I liked 'Wedding Bells' but it wasn't quite right. When I heard 'Lovesick Blues' I went bananas. That's the way it hit everyone who ever heard it. I went mad on it; so they got the record out and took the number off it for me. I went to a place in Robson Street and gave them the number. I got one of the first pressings of the record. The girl in the shop started getting me catalogues. I couldn't wait for Saturdays so I could get to the record shop and spend my one an' nine on a record. I bought every single Hank Williams record."

Bernie Green tells a similar story.

"I first started playing music when I was about 12 (1950) when I first heard Hank Williams and Jimmie Rogers. We didn't have a radiogram at home but a friend of mine had some records and an old gramophone. He put on some records and one of them was Hank Williams. From that moment, as soon as I heard that, I was bitten by the bug. I knew as soon as I heard it that that was what I was going to do. I found a place where they sold records and the woman there was very knowledgeable. It was the Music Box on West Derby Road, run by a woman called Dianne and her mother. They were very helpful and told me what was available—Carl

Phil Brady at the Brick Wall Country Festival, 1992. (photo F. Hunt)

7

Smith, Webb Pierce, Hank Williams, Lefty Frizzell. I couldn't stop listening to them.

"It seemed everyone was a guitar player, so of course I just had to have a guitar, which me Mam got me from a shop in Manchester Street that sold second-hand guitars. Me Mam bought me one for about £4 or £5, which was a veritable fortune.

"I got to know another lad, Roy Fleetwood, who was playing and singing. He in turn knew another lad, Snowy, who was much older than us. He was familiar with all the Jimmie Rogers songs, although he hadn't heard of Hank Williams. I brought Hank Williams to him. We just gelled, even though there was a vast age difference.

"Every night when I came home from school and he came home from work I'd be at his house and I'd have whatever record I'd managed to get hold of and he would show me the chords that went with it. We stayed together for many years. With Roy and Snowy I started a little trio and we played little pubs and clubs. Then we had another lad with us—Bobby Prior, a rhythm guitarist and singer—and we formed a little band called The Drifting Cowboys, after Hank Williams' band. I was about 14 or 15 then (around 1953).

"In those early days there were no drummers so the line-up consisted of Roy Fleetwood on steel guitar (known then as Hawaiian guitar), Snowy on lead guitar, Bobby Prior on rhythm, and me on rhythm and vocals."

Tony Barnes got interested at around the same time but in a slightly different way.

"Before I knew of anyone else here, I was interested in country. It started around the end of 1952. A cousin of mine used to get up and listen to the American (Armed) Forces Network. He put me on to it, so I got up at five every morning. The show started at five past five until half past. You could hear all the records that you couldn't get here. Saturday morning was the 'American Country Top Seven'. You couldn't buy the records here but then I got to know fellas who were going to sea and I asked them to bring certain records home. Eventually you got to know fellas who've got the same likings as yourself."

So it would appear that country music began to make an impression among a very select group of people in Liverpool from the early 1950s. Hank Walters and The Dusty Road Ramblers, together with The Drifting

Cowboys and Phil Brady's Ranchers, were all playing pubs and clubs around the city but it appears to have been very low key and on a small scale. Typically, Hank Walters has strong views as to what led to the country scene taking off in a much bigger way.

"The Black Cat kicked country music off as such in Liverpool. See, before that we were doing a few working men's clubs but there was nothing regular anywhere until The Black Cat took off. You won't find any country music clubs anywhere in Britain as long ago as that."

The Black Cat, run by Walters and his band, opened on 12 February, 1957, and existed for around ten years. Hank's view of it as being the first country club, central to the development of the scene in the city, is a view echoed by many others.

However, it could be that this is a misleading view, as Bernie Green explains:

"The Black Cat was important in Liverpool, but although there's a lot of talk about it being the first country club, in fact it wasn't. There was a fella named Carl Noviski, who was a local lad, who got in touch with me. I'd only be around 15 or 16 then (around 1954). He was looking for help. He put an advert in The Echo saying 'Anyone interested in country music'. We had a meeting at a restaurant in town and I went along. There was Carl Noviski; Dianne, the girl from the record shop (The Music Box); and four or five others including Bob Sedden. He doesn't play but he's a great collector. Carl was delighted to learn that I was in a band and we kept in touch.

"We then got around to hiring a little hall. It was a little Labour Club in Kensington, Dean Road. We hired that; my band played at it and Carl did the organising—putting posters out and organising the door. We put an advert in The Echo and the first night it was packed and the second night you couldn't get in. We ran it for three or four months and it was a sell out every time, so we decided to get a bigger hall. We came down to Islington where there was a big hall above the shops that held 200 to 300 people. That was packed every time—it was a big success. We were surprised to find that there were so many lovers of country music.

"I had by this time a reasonable collection of country records and that was what it all seemed to be about. People were amazed to find that you had this Hank Snow record or that Lefty Frizzell record and they'd lend you

9

Kenny Johnson, voted best male performer 1993 (BMCA). (photo Jim Silverman)

what they had. This was of course good for learning new songs. That was a complete success and the next thing was that Walters contacted me.

"When The Black Cat came along, country music was already established in this area. Carl Noviski went out of country music into soul music. I was playing all the time and didn't have time to be running the club. I've always kicked myself—I should have kept it going. We did have a name for the club, but I can't recall it. It was 30 years ago."

In short, then, country music seems to have taken off in Liverpool from around 1950, with the first groups emerging in the early years of the decade. But the success of the early ventures by Hank Walters and Bernie Green indicates that just below the surface there was a large audience of committed country fans waiting for something to happen.

Elsewhere in the UK, country music was all but invisible.

The opening of The Black Cat in 1957 ushered in an explosion of new country bands, like The Kentuckians, The Miller Brothers and The Blue Mountain Boys. Eventually this led to the opening of more venues such as Ossie Wade's (also known as Walton Lane Social Club) and the 21 Club in Croxteth.

Of course, country music did not exist in a vacuum. The late Fifties also saw the rise of skiffle, as Hank Walters describes:

"In 1955/56, Lonnie Donegan came along with skiffle. I reckon he had more influence on country music and rock music in this town than anything else. Music was evolving from America with Presley and so on and our beat, or the Merseybeat, was evolving and it had a distinct sound of its own."

Alan Clayson, writing in his recent biography of George Harrison, describes the influence of country on skiffle in 1950s Liverpool:

"Merseyside had more of a country and western bias: understandably so because within the area abounded more such artists than anywhere outside Nashville. On any given weekend you could guarantee that plenty of the three-hundred-odd venues affiliated to the Liverpool Social Club Association had booked The Dusty Road Ramblers, The Hillsiders, The Ranchers and any others from a legion of outfits playing the kinda music folk liked tappin' a foot to. Notable among young skifflers favouring a C&W approach were The Blue Mountain Boys, who adopted the 'hard' style of the legendary Hank Williams." [1]

Kenny Johnson's first group (made up of friends from the same street in Speke) were The Black Jack Skiffle Group and he recalls the first live music he ever heard being that of Lonnie Donegan.

Eddie Clayton, once of The Dusty Road Ramblers and now in Joe Rogers Country, formed The Eddie Clayton Skiffle Group in 1957, with his next door neighbour from the Dingle, named Richie Starkey—later of course to be known as Ringo Starr. Clayton's real name was Eddie Miles but this changed because, as Alan Clayson reported in his book on *Ringo Starr*, "Clayton rolled off the tongue easier than Miles and looked better symmetrically. It also had more 'down home' connotations." [2]

Country bands often played on the same bill as The Beatles and other Merseybeat bands and there was definitely some cross-fertilisation, as Spencer Leigh notes in *Country Music Round Up*, May 1981: "If you look at Merseybeat bands' repertoires, there was a lot of country songs in there. There was a great country/pop crossover." [3]

Hank Walters recalls playing at The Cavern at the same time as The Beatles. "We were on The Cavern one night (about 1960) and of course we didn't have pounding guitars and lots of noise. I came on stage and said 'Ladies and Gentlemen...' and a big roar went up because they were only youngsters, 'Ladies and Gentlemen, we don't play rock and roll, we don't play anything fancy. We just play country music and if you don't like it...' Well, I blew a raspberry. They all loved it and we couldn't go wrong after that. The owner of The Cavern went a bundle on us and we were doing The Cavern in them days about once every three weeks after that."

As Walters told Spencer Leigh in the same *Country Music Round Up* article: "Some of the groups used to come in for a bevy (at The Black Cat) when they were just getting going. I remember one time we'd done a show and John Lennon said, 'I don't go much on your music lad, but give us your hat'. I told him I didn't think much of their music, come to that, and I didn't think they'd get anywhere unless they got on with it and played country.

"All The Beatles came to The Black Cat and I used to tell them that I could hear bits of country in what they were doing. They were listening to us, so we must have influenced them." [4]

Songs like "What Goes On" from the *Rubber Soul* LP bear this out. Ringo Starr takes the vocal on this track and indeed gets a rare writing credit on the song, alongside Lennon and McCartney.

Tony Barnes, The Black Cat compere, clearly remembers The Beatles' drummer at the club.

"John Banks was on the door at The Black Cat. He came over one night and said 'Tony, you're wanted at the door' and it was Ringo with my cousin Roy Trafford (who with Ringo had been in The Eddie Clayton Skiffle Group) wanting to be signed in. I announced from the stage that it was nice to have Ringo Starr in the audience and he got a big clap. He'd joined The Beatles by then. Richie's a great lover of country music."

Indeed, after The Beatles split, Starr recorded *Beaucoup of Blues* (1970 Apple), an album of country and western tunes, despite the fact that the music was "the squarest, most right wing genre in pop." (5)

Completed in six days, *Beaucoup of Blues* is, according to Bob Wolfinden in *The Beatles Apart*, "One of the best Beatles solo albums. Ringo's homely, lugubrious voice suited those typically maudlin country songs like a charm." (6)

Tony Allen, lead singer with The Blue Mountain Boys, gives a very realistic appraisal of how it felt to be a country band at the time when The Beatles were first starting to make their mark. Allen's band released their only single, "Drop Me Gently" b/w "One Small Photograph," on Oriole records in 1962. "It caused quite a stir because we were actually the first country band to do a recording. At the same time, The Beatles' "Love Me Do" came out and we just got lost. As good as we were, we were just too old.

"We started doing the clubs again like everybody else. We were voted Best Country Band in England for 1962. The presentation was made at, I think, The Majestic Ballroom in Birkenhead. All the various groups who'd won something from *Mersey Beat* were there. I'd seen The Beatles many times before, but this time was the first time they did 'Please Please Me' live. I said to the band that we may as well pack up, because that song was

'Little' Bernie Green with the Everglades at the Brick Wall, 1992. (photo F. Hunt)

13

The Hillsiders, Country Music Association (GB) 1971-73 Best Group of the Year

going to be the next number one. The others were saying, 'Oh, it'll just disappear like "Love Me Do."'

"What happened was that they (the record companies) tried to make everybody else sound like The Beatles. But they were originals, one-offs never to be repeated. In all that kerfuffle, good groups got lost. It killed people's awareness of other music.

"Now country music had done very well in Liverpool at that time. There were that many groups that I can't remember them all. But then it became The Beatles Era and we started to get lost a little. We weren't getting much work."

But country musicians were also affected in a positive way by the Merseybeat boom. After leaving school in 1950, Joe Butler (formerly of The Hillsiders) joined a group called The Country Four, which also included Kenny Johnson. Johnson left and formed a rock group called The Cascades.

"Kenny asked me to play bass guitar for Sonny Webb and The Cascades," recalls Butler. "We went through the Sixties Merseybeat thing, although Kenny and I were always into country music."

(Indeed Kenny Johnson got his stage name of "Sonny Webb" from the names of two famous country artists, Sonny James and Webb Pierce.)

"When the Sixties thing died down, with people like The Beatles and Gerry Marsden leaving town, we thought if we're going to be skint we may as well be skint playing music we really want to play, which was country. We changed the name to The Hillsiders and it's been that way for 25 years.

"Merseybeat helped country a lot. From some of the Merseybeat bands, we got some great country players. They didn't know what country was, but they got to listen to it and realising they could play it, they started joining country bands. I've travelled all over the UK and Liverpool bands definitely play with more meat behind the music. They tend to attack the music a lot more. Out of town they tend to be very 'pretty sounding' with a front line singer and a backing band. But Liverpool seems to have taken the Merseybeat thing a stage further and you get about three or four singers in a band and they really play a bit harder. And probably they will tackle more obscure material than the rest of the country, because Liverpool people are known for the fact that they'll listen to anything as long as it's played well, whereas out of town they want to hear the usual hits."

Kenny Johnson reinforces this view. "The Hillsiders started around 1964/65. The Beatles had all gone. I noticed that the younger generation didn't want to know. The crowds that had followed us (The Cascades)

Raconteur, vocalist, guitarist Jerry Devine in a pensive mood at the Atlantic, 1992. (photo F. Hunt)

15

around weren't going to the clubs any more. All their favourites had gone—The Searchers, Billy J Kramer. Then there was a new influx with younger bands coming in—The Crying Shames, The Escorts, that type of thing. The youngsters wanted them. We were too old for them. We weren't really cutting mustard any more.

"We went to Ireland on a trip and we all got into Buck Owens and when we came back we said that's what we want to do. We might as well just play country music like Buck Owens and George Jones. Let's just go totally country. Frankie Wan got a pedal steel, Brian Hilton came in, and we became The Hillsiders.

"It was forced on us, really, to go full country because we weren't doing it any more, and the new rock stars had come in and that was it. But it was good fun while it lasted and it put us in good stead too as the basis for the Buck Owens thing. That Sixties rock gave us a lot of edge on the other bands in the country and The Hillsiders were tops for say ten years.

"That was the Liverpool Country Sound. There were quite a few bands around when we came on, but when they saw us I think they changed. A lot of them went and got pedal steel guitars, which nobody had. We were the first pedal steel band. I think we really were a shot in the arm, because a lot of bands started appearing just because we were getting big crowds."

Everything Country: Pat and Gerry Allen's shop on Aigburth Road, 1992

16

Women have played a very important role in country music in Liverpool over the last thirty years.

Pat Allen is known by everyone on the local country circuit and has had a constant influence on the scene by way of the long-established Pat and Gerry Allen's country record shop (Gerry was Pat's late husband).

As we have already seen, Joan Goldby worked closely with her husband, Carl, in promoting country music at Ossie Wade's and elsewhere, as well as singing with him in various groups. They are one of a number of couples who were brought together by country music, as Joan explains.

"The Blue Mountain Boys' first job was at Butlin's Filey, where I first met Carl because I was on the staff as a Bluecoat. We fell in love and I followed him to Liverpool."

Carl and Joan married in 1962, and they played together in a number of different bands after The Blue Mountain Boys split up. These bands included Carl Goldie's Country Sounds, Tradewinds, and finally up until 1977 as just Carl and Joan Goldie. After this, they moved to South Africa for business reasons, but they still found time to perform occasionally. The pair are now living in Carlisle.

Bunter Perkins also met his wife, Nora, when The Blue Mountain Boys played at Butlin's Filey in 1961.

"The first day we were there I went up to the bar where she was working, and she asked what sort of music we played. When I told her it was country, she said, 'Have we got to listen to that all summer?' I told her if she didn't like it, she could sod off. I told everyone else not to go near her, but eventually we got chatting and it went from there."

Tony Allen, also of The Blue Mountain Boys, met his wife, Rikki, at Butlin's Filey and they continued as a very successful duo, touring all over the world until the late 1970s.

Although it is clear that there have always been a number of female country singers, the early years of country in Liverpool seem to have been almost completely dominated by men.

The female singers like Joan Goldby, Rikki Allen, and Patsy Foley began to emerge around the mid-1960s. Patsy Foley is often referred to as

Liverpool's Patsy Cline or Liverpool's Queen of Country. Foley was born in 1940 and brought up in Liverpool in the Scotland Road area, where she began playing guitar and singing.

In 1958 she won a competition on the Isle of Man that gave her the opportunity to do a season with Ivy Benson's 17-piece all-girl band. When she returned from this, she was asked to join The Blue Mountain Boys.

"Everyone knows me from playing at The Temple with Bunter Perkins and The Blue Mountain Boys. There's only me, and Bunter, and Gerry Devine left.

"I'm not the best, but I am the oldest. I tend to sing the older Patsy Cline, Joan Shepherd, and the old-fashioned stuff.

"The other country bands are a good lot. If I go along and see them, I've got to get up and sing. I couldn't refuse them but they would never not ask me."

Other female singers around today in Liverpool include Jody Stephens, Carol Weston, and Patsy Lee. And of course there are The Arcadian Ladies: Clare, Pauline, and Lorna, the three daughters of Hank Walters, who have been playing regularly with their father since the beginning of 1992. They have begun to write their own songs, and they have already earned a reputation as an excellent live act.

The Arcadian Ladies: Claire, Pauline and Lorna, in Bootle, 1992.
(photo C. Farley)

Although Bernie Green's country club may have predated it, The Black Cat is generally regarded as the first British country club of any note. Who better to tell the story of the venue than its founder, Hank Walters, who played there every week with The Dusty Road Ramblers?

"The Black Cat opened on the 12th of February 1957...now you won't find any country music in Britain as long ago as that. It was called The Country Jamboree Club and it was on the top floor of Sampson and Barlow's in London Road. It held about 200 and we used to really cram them in.

"It was a Corporation Club. No one was going to the club because of where it was situated, so we asked them if we could have it on a Friday night. We didn't have any money to put it in the papers—we just opened it. We got a copying machine and we made a load of things and put them up in The Mechano, Tate and Lyle's, Bibby's and all over the place. Our mates went and got them stuck up. The night it opened, the queue went right down London Road and round towards the bloody Gaumont. We got choc a bloc.

"It ran from 1957 to about 1967 and we played every Friday. We'd have guest bands. Kenny Johnson came on in a guest spot, with Sonny Webb and The Cascades. It was very successful. Very seldom could you walk up and get a space in there. The Black Cat (as it was later renamed) kicked country music off in Liverpool."

Tony Barnes was the compere at the club.

"I was going there before it was The Black Cat, back when it was The Country Jamboree Club and the compere was Charlie Dix. Eventually Ralph (Hank Walters) asked me to take over.

"Later on a fella called Les Ackley got the rights to The Country Jamboree Club and he changed the name to the Black Cat Club. He didn't interfere in any other way.

"Country fans from near and wide came to it...a lot of lads from over the water as well as other musicians. Hank's band played most weeks and a lot of guest artists used to get up each week: Bobby Brooks, Kenny Page, some weeks the Miller Brothers would come along. We usually tried to have two acts every week—Hank and someone else."

Everyone involved in the local country scene had a comment about The Black Cat.

Tony Allen (Blue Mountain Boys): "It was a place to go where you could hear live country music. We got paid a pittance and it was a pittance that they charged on the door."

Bunter Perkins (a member of Walters' band when the club opened): "It was a great place to play. You wouldn't believe the

Bunter Perkins, out of retirement and playing again, 1992. (photo C. Farley)

amount of people we got in there. We called them 'underground people' because there had been nowhere for them to go—they were all in their houses listening to this stuff and then the club opened up.

"We did the whole night and we had a break when we just played country records. We had two girls who used to take the money at The Cavern. We used to give them five shillings each to come and take the money on the door. I think we used to charge people about half a crown. One of them came up to me and said she had a brother called Sonny Webb (Kenny Johnson) who wanted to have a go on stage with his band. I spoke to Hank about it and said why don't we get them up, give them a fiver and it will give us a break. So we did.

"We got a contract for Butlin's so we passed it (the main spot) over to Johnno and we told him what we made on the door (around £60) and he went mad because we'd only been giving him a fiver."

Paddy Kelly: "The Black Cat was magic. It was all like Johnny Cash, Hank Snow, Buck Owens. You'd see a seven-piece band on stage—all out of different bands, but all playing together. You'd walk in with your guitar and you'd get up and play. A magic atmosphere—you'll never see that again. It happens a lot in Nashville. It used to happen here but not any more."

20

Mick O'Toole, a local enthusiast, gives a punter's view of The Black Cat. "It was a very small place. You had to go upstairs, which was a bind for everyone, especially coming down if you were half pissed. It was a nuisance for the bands because they had to carry their gear up. Great atmosphere, great fun."

The success of The Black Cat led to the opening of other country clubs, notable among them the 21 Club and Ossie Wade's. The 21 Club on Croxteth Road was owned by George Bolt and ran every Thursday with Gordon Fleming and the Miller Brothers as the resident acts.

Ossie Wade's, on the corner of Spellow Lane and Walton Lane, was another regular venue, owned by Ada Wade with Tony Barnes once again taking on the role of compere.

Carl and Joan Goldby promoted Sunday night country events at Ossie Wade's and they recall giving The Hillsiders their first booking there.

"They repeated a couple of songs because they'd only learnt about six numbers. They were so good that people wouldn't let them get off."

According to Carl, Ossie Wade's was the first club to actively promote country music.

Veteran country artist Paddy Kelly, with his daughters

Carl and Joan Goldby, left, with Hobo Rick (Ricky Tomlinson) at Ossie Wade's, circa 1962

"The Black Cat did promote country music, but it wasn't done for that purpose. It was done for Hank and his band. Mind you, they did put the Miller Boys on and anyone else around. Hank must have everything due to him because from the early days he was the one that really pushed country music, up until the time I took it a step further and tried to spread it around and commercialise it.

"We tried to get several venues to try to push the music, but it never took off anywhere else. I think if we'd managed to get our own premises and really promote it as a country venue, then I think that would have done very well. At Ossie Wade's we used to hire the night—they'd take the bar and we'd take the door. Everybody thought we were making a fortune but at five bob a time and the groups wanting more money.... We just paid the band out of the door—there was very little left. The average fee was below £20. Normally it was around £12.

"We obviously did it as a business. No matter how keen you are on the music, it's got to be a business as well. You do hear a couple of accusations here and there about us being wide boys, but everybody who makes money is a wide boy. Ossie's used to break even. There were nights when it was absolutely choc a bloc—when Tammy Wynette came over, for instance, and we backed her with The Ranchers. She came back from somewhere in

Widnes and did Ossie's. We brought Tommy Collins back to Ossie's as well. You could squeeze 200 in at a maximum. Charlie on the door would be saying 'No more...Its choc a bloc in there, you can't get any more in'. We always turned people away when we opened up. It was highly successful."

Goldby was also involved in the setting up of the North West Country Music Association, although it appears the idea originated with Tony Barnes, as Barnes explains:

"From what I could see, we (the country musicians) weren't getting anywhere—there was no argument—we just weren't getting anywhere. The idea (for the association) was to keep the money inside the bands rather than working through agents. We could have been our own agency. (The association) gave the fellas a chance to meet each other and any new people who applied got a chance to get to know the already existing bands.

"I can't remember how long it lasted. I'll make a guess—two years—but I've really no idea. I was the secretary of the association. The money was thirty bob a man. That was poor money even then. At the time there was no interest in money—it was secondary to the music."

Bernie Green sums up the short-lived association very succinctly: "The idea was for all the bands to join in, get together and promote the music. But associations being associations, they started branching off."

Despite the collapse of the North West Country Music Association, the strength of the country scene in Liverpool in the mid-1960s can be gauged by the success of a series of large festival shows organised by Goldby, who set up his own agency to promote country music in the city.

The first "Festival of Country Music Show" took place in 1964 at the Philharmonic Hall with a 1,700-capacity audience in attendance. It featured The Hillsiders, Phil Brady and The Ranchers, Hank Walters and the Dusty Road Ramblers, Goldby's own band, Country Sounds, as well as Pete Sayers from London, and Bill Crofton (an American Blue Grass artist). Goldby explains the background to these shows:

"We organised it right from the ground up—did all the work on it. Nothing like that had been done before, so we were intent on doing it.

"Then we did three Grafton shows and we called them 'Liverpool Goes Country'. That was Tony Barnes's idea for the title. They were quite

23

Booming in the Sixties, today the 21 Club sits silent on Croxteth Road. (photo F. Hunt)

successful. Two were lock outs and the other one broke even. Then we did the likes of the Crane Theatre, The Rialto and two cruises on the Royal Iris."

Carl and Joan Goldby were also behind what was billed as "The First National Country Music Package Tour," which took place in August 1965. It was headlined by American artist Tommy Collins and his wife Wanda. The rest of the bill was made up of The Hillsiders (then signed to Pye Records), Phil Brady and the Ranchers (signed to Decca), Carl Goldie's Country Sounds (Decca) and Hank Walters and the Dusty Road Ramblers (Decca). The compere for the tour was Hobo Rick (actor Ricky Tomlinson), a regular on the Liverpool country circuit.

Goldby takes up the story: "Tommy Collins had been a number one artist who was then in a bit of a slide in his career. He was still a big name in England, so we booked him. The show wasn't a success at all. During the promotion time I took ill so we didn't get much promotion done. We lost a lot of money out of that. Apart from that it was a success in every other way. The communication between the British and the American artists was great. We all went on a coach—all going into pubs with our instruments. We were late getting to Glasgow because we couldn't get them out of the pub. To make matters worse, the brakes on the coach were faulty

24

and as soon as we hit a hill the driver had to start pumping the brakes. Still, it was almost worth losing your shirt for.

"We did Liverpool, Newcastle and Glasgow. We had two other shows booked but we had to cancel them because the advance ticket sales were terrible.

"Tommy Collins wasn't a very well-known name. The difference later on when Mervin Con came on the scene and asked us to help promote the Johnny Cash show was that Cash was still a big name then. We were supposed to get half the profits but we never got a cent out of it, although we did get to spend the day with Johnny Cash at the Adelphi Hotel.

"We were intent on making them (the festivals) regular events, but as soon as we got them off the ground, Mervin Con came in from London with pots of money and wiped the floor with us."

It was during this same (mid-1960s) period that the country groups began to make records as well. As already mentioned, the honour of making the area's first country record went to The Blue Mountain Boys with "One Small Photograph" b/w "Drop Me Gently," which was released on Oriole Records (one of the first small local independent labels) in 1962. They were signed by John Schroeder after they bluffed their way into an audition for the label at the Manchester Apollo Theatre. (Incidentally, in 1963 Schroeder returned to Liverpool with a mobile unit to record 'any band that contacted him'. These sessions resulted in two volumes of This Is Mersey Beat, which sold 15,000 copies each in the UK and included four tracks by Sonny Webb and The Cascades.

The contract from Oriole arrived while The Blue Mountain Boys were playing at Butlin's Clacton on Sea. At this stage, Bernie Green (generally known as 'Little Bernie') was the singer, but Tony Allen (the group's original vocalist) was also present, working in the personnel department of the camp. He recalls how the record came about.

"Halfway through the season, a recording contract arrived from John Schroeder at Oriole Records. The first song they offered the band was 'Itsy, Bitsy, Teeny, Weeny', which was totally unsuitable, and the other one was 'Wolverton Mountain', which Claude King had done in the States (where it sold a million). The Blue Mountain Boys were to do a cover job.

"They (the band) had a disagreement with Bernie and the outcome was that they came back to me. I got permission for two nights off my job to go

Country Music Program

Liverpool Echo
The talent spotter's all talk sadly of the shortage of good musical acts, there are a few however and among them **Rikki Allen**, who sings with her husband **Tony**, accompanying her on the guitar, **Rikki** is an electrifying personality with a flair for comedy, as well as both having superb voices.

Club News Frankfurt
Member's are being entertained to the fullest this week, with the **Rikki & Tony Allen Show**, these two entertainers are from the British Isles and are tops in Ballads, Country & Western tunes mixed with Comedy and antics.

Icelandic Advertiser
Rikki & Tony hail from the British Isles they bang out Country & Western music and comedy and keep the audience clamouring for encores.

Berlin Observer
Country & Western highlights this weeks entertainments with two great personalities, **Rikki & Tony Allen** who hail from England and sing the Nashville Sound, they are immensely popular wherever they go.

Here they are -
The greatest
Country & Western act
in Europe

Rikki and Tony Allen

Rikki & Tony

ROYAL NAVAL ASS. CLUB LTD.
Mill Brow, Widnes

JUBILEE COUNTRY SHOW

with

HANK WALTERS
DUSTY ROAD RANDLERS
THE MILLER BOYS
THE KENTUCKIANS

on Friday, 10th June 1977

Commencing— 8.00p.m.

Free L.P. Raffle   Refreshments Available

Ticket 75p

Jubilee Country Show ticket

and sing with them. In the end I had to make a decision. Butlin's had offered me a chance to go to Pwllheli to be the personnel manager. Anyhow, I decided I'd stay with the band.

"We'd rehearsed 'Wolverton Mountain' but then the American publishers withdrew their permission to cover it. So he (Schroeder) offered us a Hank Thompson song called 'Drop Me Gently,' which was done in a waltz tempo, and an Australian song called 'One Small Photograph'. We did 'Photograph' in two takes and 'Drop Me Gently' in one. We heard it played back and we all got £28. Billy Cooper signed for the royalties."

"We were in France (playing at an American base) when it was released," Bunter Perkins recalls. "When we heard it we thought they'd ruined it because they'd added strings and the piano on later."

As already noted, the record did well, but the Beatles, with the release of "Love Me Do," stole the thunder. However, the record is still requested on a regular basis on local radio today, and it undoubtedly captures the feel and sound of the time.

Carl Goldby, another member of The Blue Mountain Boys, believes a potential number one was snatched away from them.

"The Blue Mountain Boys almost made it. They won a competition that was being run by Curry's and Radio Luxembourg. They won the competition with 'Orange Blossom Special,' which was an instrumental. I think the prize was a portable radio, but they asked if they could have an echo unit for the band instead. They were going to record 'Orange Blossom' but then The Sputniks did it and they went straight to number one."

Goldby was also involved in the Liverpool Goes Country compilation LP released on Rex Records (part of Decca) in 1965. The LP featured tracks from Tom O'Connor, Phil Brady and the Ranchers, Hank Walters and The Dusty Road Ramblers and Carl Goldie's Country Sounds. A four-track EP with the same Liverpool Goes Country title was released by Carl Goldie's Country Sounds at the same time.

The Hillsiders have had the most sustained recording career of the Liverpool country bands, releasing over 15 albums and many singles during their 25-year career.

"There were a couple of songs which did well," Kenny Johnson remembers. "We got a lot of airplay and were verging on chart success.

27

We did Ray Davies's 'Days' and then The Kinks brought it out as a single when they found out we were doing it. And of course it was a hit for them and not for us. Also we recorded 'Love of the Common People' and 'Gently On My Mind,' which were then hits for other people. We had quite a few which were on the verge of breaking through."

Hank Walters has recorded three LPs and an EP during his long career. He remembers how one of his first recording attempts brought him into contact with The Rolling Stones.

"The Hillsiders got us to go down to London to record something. The young band in the studio before us were taking ages and I had a bit of an argument with them. We recorded four songs in twenty minutes, all in one take, which impressed the other band. They brought us back some chips because they'd kept us waiting. They turned out to be The Rolling Stones and they asked us to do a gig with them in Norwich."

(Hank also supported another rock legend when he played with Marc Bolan in Southport).

Nowadays the only Liverpool country artists releasing records on anything like a regular basis are The Hillsiders, Kenny Johnson and Northwind, and, to a lesser extent, The Paddy Kelly Band (who are all well known on the national circuit). Most local groups do, however, make cassettes which they sell at their performances.

"Until recently, country music enjoyed a unique status somewhere between that of Big Cult and Big Joke. The faithful dressed up in ten-gallon hats and rhinestones and made the pilgrimage to Nashville or the Wembley Festival of Country Music: the rest of us mostly smiled at this adult pantomime of sentimental naivete, old fashioned music and kitsch Americana...Now country is serious business again." [7]

This quote comes from Robert Sandall in *The Sunday Times*, September 1992, attempting to explain the recent revival of interest in country music in Britain. It is a situation that echoes what is taking place in America where country is now in many ways bigger than rock music. An entirely new roster of country talent, such as Garth Brooks (who at one point in 1993 had four albums in the U.S. top twenty), Sonny Tritt and Clint Black have expanded the audience for country music and are among the most well-known names in American pop music today. These singers are generally young and good looking, with the old redneck image now largely a thing of the past. Their approach is much more eclectic than that of the earlier purists, with soft rock, blues and gospel creeping into arrangements.

An example of this is Billy Ray Cyrus, who is regarded as a country artist, but whose "country hit" "Achy, Breaky Heart," a British number one single, could as easily be classified as soft rock.

The most plausible reason for this upsurge in the popularity of the genre would appear to lie with American radio, which has disenfranchised whole sections of the public, with rock stations moving towards a harder sound, and black stations often opting for an all out-rap format. Country stations, by way of contrast, can offer some comfort for the great mass of people searching for melodic "proper" pop songs with real tunes and lyrics.

In America, there are now more stations devoted to country (about 2,500) than for any other format and the country revival has crucially depended upon these.

In the UK, the country revival has no real home on the airwaves, outside of specialist programmes on local stations in country strongholds like Liverpool, East Anglia and Humberside. In Liverpool, Joe Butler's country show on Radio City has been running for almost twenty years, while *Sounds*

Country on Radio Merseyside has been on the airwaves for almost thirty years, first with Don Allan, then Billy Butler and for the last 17 years with Kenny Johnson.

But even if there was a specialist country show on every local radio station, the cultural obstacle to country's wider acceptance would still remain, as Sandall explains in the Times article.

"However much we might admire the crafting of those songs about marital break up in Oklahoma and whisky-fuelled infidelities in Austin, country music remains the folk music of white working class America....The only other sort of pop music which sells this big in the States and equally poorly abroad is rap...the authentic and often incomprehensible voice of poor black America...Like rap, like all genuine folk music in fact, country will travel, but it can't be transplanted." [8]

Whether country music will ever enjoy mainstream success in Britain remains to be seen, but what of the situation in Liverpool today, and what are the prospects for the future?

Can the recent spark of interest that Sandall mentions rekindle the Liverpool country scene?

If you open up The Liverpool Echo Leisure Guide on any Friday, there are always a small number of local country artists still appearing in the city's pubs. There are regular country nights at places like The Tent in Huyton, The Brickwall in Tarbock, the MAA Club in Sheil Road and residencies with old favourites like The Bar Room Boys playing The Hangman in Bank Hall every Sunday and The Union on Commercial Road every Monday. An advert for Joe Rogers' Country (which also features George Neild and Eddie Clayton) at The Union simply states "George and the Boys," but this is enough to pack the pub out every week with regulars eager to see this bunch of old stalwarts, regarded by many locals as the best in the business, go through their paces. And Hank Walters is certain to be appearing somewhere with his three daughters, now known as The Arcadian Ladies.

Indeed, Walters seems as good a place as any to start when looking for reflections on the state of country music in Liverpool today.

"It's still there...What it is now, it's taken for granted, like Scouse. It'll never, ever go away now. The scene is healthy but it's taken for granted."

Another veteran, Paddy Kelly, has a different perspective:

"The country music scene in Liverpool at the moment is really down. There's a lot of good bands here but no venues for them to play. There's no money in Liverpool, plus there's so many acts now that people can take their pick. The venues are closing down and we're all competing against singers with taped backing.

"The Dock Road was the killer. When that opened up and those pubs got a one o'clock license—a lot of the country bands went to play there and the (country) clubs were suffering. So the clubs had to look for different entertainers because they couldn't get the country bands. When the Dock Road finished, some of the clubs didn't want the country bands back.

"There's not many of us left. There's Hank Walters, Bernie Green, us....As George Jones sang, 'Who's going to fill their shoes'. There's no one to fill our shoes. There's a lot of young bands but they seem to tire of country music very quickly and change their image and go on to something else.

"I just hope country music will come back in Liverpool, the way it was in the late Sixties, early Seventies. It was a magic scene. I've still got a few years left in me and I'm sure the likes of Hank Walters, Kenny Johnson, and

The new generation: Darren Neild with Joe Rogers Country at the Union, 1992. (photo F. Hunt)

The Hillsiders will be going for a few years yet. But sadly there's no new bands coming up. I'd love to see a young band and be able to go to them and give them the benefit of my experience."

This is a view shared by Kenny Johnson, who in his position as country DJ and singer with Northwind is as well placed as any to comment.

"The scene now in Liverpool has dropped. It's nowhere near what it used to be. But the man in the street hasn't got the money. Once the depression has lifted maybe you'll see an upsurge in the clubs again.

"I think it is dying at the moment. There's no new blood—not to warrant another twenty years anyway. You can't see who is coming up and there's not the same opportunities now. And you've got the thing where if you're not established they don't want to know you—but how are you going to get established?

"There's not many venues...The Liverpool country scene compared to what it used to be is finished. It's dead. You've got maybe four regular venues. There's pubs, but we haven't got major clubs anywhere. The Old Swan Conservative Club, The Brickwall, Orrell Park Ballroom, St. Aloysious..that's it. There should be more than that for the size of the city. We'll just have to wait and see if the tide turns with time. If I have a night off, I'll take in some of the others, but I haven't seen any good young bands."

Bernie Green (still playing with The Everglades) has a similar point of view:

"The unfortunate thing is that there's not so many young lads coming into it now. When (Gary) Potter came along and Darren Neild (now in UK Country), Davy Whitehead (Joe Piper band), Lenny Whitehead (Ben Rees Band), Melvin Duffy, they were all the younger element. That was excellent for us older fellas to see. One night these fellas were all jamming together in a pub and one of them turned to me and said 'See, it's in good hands'. That stands out in my memory. Each one of them was superb in his own right and still is. But there doesn't seem to be any other young ones coming along. But it can't die out because someone, somewhere will come along. It's good that Hank Walters has got his daughters with him now—I can remember them when they were kids."

It is undoubtedly true that there is a lack of young performers today and the reason is probably a simple one. Most teenagers are far more likely to be exposed to pop and dance music through radio, TV and discos than to country. The exception seems to be when young musicians are brought up in a home environment where country music is the norm.

As a young lad, Gary Potter (who is only 25 now) played country music with his father in venues like The Bramley Moore on the Dock Road, as John Caldwell (landlord and resident musician at The Atlantic Pub) remembers.

"He used to amaze everyone. A great country guitar player, but he got into jazz pretty fast."

Gary Potter stills plays regularly at The Atlantic on the Dock Road (to packed and very appreciative audiences) but his talent has been lost from country music.

Until recently, two of John Neild's sons play with him in UK Country, with Darren (21) on vocals and Paul (19) on drums. The Neilds are a country family through and through, with John's older brother George one of the city's best known country singers and still playing with the very popular Joe Rogers' Country. John and George's nephew, Kevin McGarry, is the singer with The Hillsiders, probably the best known of all Liverpool country bands. With such a pedigree it was perhaps inevitable that Darren

Tony Allen, formerly of The Blue Mountain Boys, in the process of building Hank's Place, 1992.

33

Orrell Park Ballroom today. (photo C. Farley)

and Paul should turn to country, as Darren explains:

"With not being brought up with the rock side of things, I never watched Top of the Pops or rock festivals or anything like that. I was brought up with country music. You couldn't put a tape on in our house without it being George's or Kevin's or his (John's). All the bands that are still around now used to come to our house, so when I started getting involved in the business they all knew me."

Paul probably gets close to the heart of the matter.

"All the family were into country and since I've been a baby I've been brought up with it, listening to it nearly every day. I've just got the taste for it and always wanted to play country."

But even in this family of country stalwarts, one of the sons, John Jr., has resisted the temptation of country and instead fronts a rock band.

So, with a lack of young performers coming up, country will undoubtedly struggle in the coming years, unless the predicted revival takes hold and American artists such as Garth Brooks manage to achieve mainstream success in Britain, thus making country more acceptable to young music enthusiasts and musicians.

The lack of venues also bodes ill for the future prospects of country in the city. Many of the Dock Road pubs where country music was once so popular have now closed down and as already noted there are few clubs left which still have a regular country night. Many pubs now rely on attractions such as karaoke machines, quiz nights, or singers with backing tapes to pull in customers, and all of these are much easier to accommodate than a band, which take up a lot of room, make a great deal of noise and require a fee at the end of the night. The only pubs where country survives (and indeed thrives) are in old-fashioned, unglamorous places like The Union and pubs such as this are getting fewer in number every month.

For the simple reason of economics, pubs and clubs will continue to put on country music if it continues to draw in the punters. Tony Allen (formerly of The Blue Mountain Boys) recently has opened a country venue called Hank's Place in West Derby. When he announced his plans on local radio, he was inundated with applications for membership.

But there is a problem here, too. It is not only Liverpool's country performers who are aging; their audiences are growing old with them. If you go to see Joe Rogers at The Union, audience and band are almost all in their fifties or older. Long-time fan Mick O'Toole reinforces this view in commenting on Rogers:

"I've been travelling to watch him for almost twenty years and the same people are in the crowd as were there twenty years ago. The band play covers of Hank Snow and other old standards, which is what the audience wants and really the whole thing could be happening in 1962, not 1992."

Bunter Perkins spotted the same thing with Patsy Foley, Liverpool's "Queen of Country."

"If you can get Patsy Foley playing with you, you can be sure of a ready-made audience. I went down to The Boathouse to see her playing and I looked around and it was like a time warp. All the people there were in The Temple (Dale Street) when we used to play there (in the late 1960s)."

Step dancing, or line dancing, which has been widely popular in the U.S., attracts an audience, but also controversy. At venues like The Orrell Park Ballroom and the Riverside Club near Southport, the audience usually dresses up in Western-style gear. In contrast to the U.S. country scene, this tends to meet with the disapproval of most country performers, who see their music being taken less seriously as a result. Bernie Green elaborates:

"I don't agree with it at all. It's derogatory to the music. The music is not about cowboys. I don't like to be a killjoy, but I don't like them to be associated with country music."

Whatever the feelings of the performers (and Bernie Green is far from being alone in these views), dancing is perhaps one way in which country music might be kept alive in Liverpool.

So at the moment the Liverpool country scene is at a critical stage. The groups and the audiences are getting older and more and more venues are shutting their doors to the music. The dancing that could attract younger audiences is frowned upon.

It appears that unless a national revival does take hold, country music is destined to move further and further towards the fringes of the city's culture and the glory days of Liverpool Country will become a distant memory.

As Kenny Johnson puts it: "We'll just have to wait and see if the tide turns with time."

Dancing at the Brick Wall Country Music Festival, 1992.

FOOTNOTES

(1)   Clayson Alan. *The Quiet One: A Life of George Harrison.* London: Sidgwick & Jackson, 1990.

(2)   Clayson Alan. *Ringo Starr: Straight Man or Joker?* London: Sidgwick & Jackson, 1991.

(3)   *Country Music Round Up*, May 1981, p. 16.

(4)   *Ibid.*

(5)   *Ibid.*

(6)   Wolfinden Bob. *The Beatles Apart.* London: Proteus Books, 1971.

(7)   Robert Sandall, *Sunday Times* 20th September 1992.

(8)   *Ibid.*

Leverhulme Sounds Series

Nashville of the North

Harmonious Relations

Forthcoming:

Dance Bands of the 30's & 40's

Irish Music in Liverpool

Music of the Black Community of Liverpool

and more........

The Leverhulme Research Team:

Dr. Sara Cohen

Kevin McManus

Tricia Jenkins

Connie Atkinson

Derek Murray

To order send £3.95 plus £2.00 p&p to

Institute of Popular Music

Box 147 University of Liverpool

Liverpool L69 3BX